This book has been provided by Mrs. Ruth Burns in memory of her Mother and Father, Louise De Tuncq - Niles and Fred Niles.

Japanese art

SPRING ART BOOKS

Japanese art

Raymond Johnes

SPRING BOOKS · LONDON

This volume is dedicated to my colleagues of the Art Circle, the Japan Society of London, and in particular to their presiding genius, Engineer-Commander A.R. Newman.

ACKNOWLEDGMENTS

The pieces and paintings in this volume are reproduced by kind permission of the following galleries and collectors: the British Museum, London (Plates 7, 8, 16, 26, 33, 34, 36, 38–47); The Hon. R.G. Erskine (Plate 1); Field Marshal Sir Francis Festing (Plates 23, 24); John Hudisteanu, Esq. (Plate 19); R. Soame Jenyns, Esq. (Plate 31); Clement Milward, Esq. (Plate 25); B.W. Robinson, Esq. (Plate 48); Mrs Mariquita Sedgwick (Plate 18); W.W.Winkworth, Esq. (Plate 25); Private Collection, London (Plates 31, 32, 33, 37); the author (Plates 2, 9, 17, 23, 24, 26, 27, 35).
The objects in Japan (Plates 3–6, 10–15, 20–22, 28–30) were photographed by the firm of Sakamoto, Tokyo, and those in London (Plates 1, 2, 7–9, 16–19, 23–27, 31–48) by David Swann, Esq.
The frontispiece illustrations, *Ink paintings* by Kano Motonobu (1476–1559) are reproduced by courtesy of the author.

1st edition 1961

2nd impression 1963

3rd impression 1964

Published by

SPRING BOOKS

Westbook House • Fulham Broadway • London

© Books for Pleasure Limited 1961

Printed in Czechoslovakia

T—1389

Contents

JAPAN

0 100 200

Miles

HOKKAIDŌ

Ū

SEA OF JAPAN

Matsushima

Sendai

KOREA

ISHIKAWA

GUMMA

Nikkō

S

N

Tōkyō
(Edo)

Kamakura

Mt Fuji ▲

Kyōto
(Heian)

HYŌGO

Ise

Izumo

H O

Sanuki

Itsukushima
(Miyajima)

Yamaguchi

Buzen
Usa

SHIKOKU

PACIFIC

Usuki

OCEAN

Higo

Nagasaki

Hiraizumi

KYŪSHŪ

SHINANO

Nagoya

L. Biwa

Azuchi

Kyōto ▲ *Hieizan*

Momoyama

Shigaraki

Kamo R. *Uji*

Nara

Kobe

KAWACHI

Asuka-Fujiwara

Hōryūji ▲ *Mt Tonómine*

Osaka

Yoshino

I

Z

A

N

A

Kōyasan ▲

Nachi

0   50

Miles

Introduction: the Background

It has too often been said that Japanese art is derivative. What artistic traditions are not? Count them: the fingers of one hand will suffice. Roman, Byzantine, Romanesque and Renaissance art are certainly not among them. But in these, as in the art of Japan, there is adaptation and a breath of originality that, without denying its parentage, can stand on its own merits.

No evidence has been discovered of a Palaeolithic culture in Japan. The earliest artifacts found are those of a Neolithic people of hunters, fishers and food-gatherers. It is presumed that these were the ancestors of the Ainu, now confined to Hokkaido, the northern island. They must already have attained this stage of civilisation when they reached southern Japan from the mainland, and until modern times, they had not progressed beyond it. Their vessels of coiled pottery have affinities with those of parallel cultures in the northern hemisphere. It is less easy to find anything comparable to their clay figures, probably of religious significance, which are exceedingly rare.

No glyptic art can be attributed with any certainty to the invaders of the Yayoi Period; they possessed the technique of the potter's wheel and kiln and worked in bronze and iron. They were no doubt of Mongolian origin and among the ancestors of the Japanese race. But it was not until they had consolidated their position that we can begin to speak of the beginnings of Japanese art.

The Dolmen Period

This period is now not believed to begin earlier than the second century A.D. As the primitive inhabitants were driven northward, agriculture and administration took root, and great tumuli similar to those found in Korea were heaped over the graves of rulers and noblemen.

Most of these tombs are regarded as sacred and few have been opened. In those that have, bronze swords and mirrors were found; also iron swords and horse-trappings with gold and silver ornament, stone beads, some of them roughly in the form of a bear's claw. Most of these are of continental, viz., of Korean types.

Cylinders of pottery were set at close intervals around the periphery of the most important tombs and, towards the end of what we may call the prehistoric period, the tops of these were ornamented with figures of men or animals. They are remarkably vivid and spontaneous works of art and they are the earliest that we can definitely designate as Japanese. A specimen is shown in Plate 1. Traditionally they are supposed to have been placed on the tombs as a substitute for human sacrifices of earlier times. During this period, the use of Chinese ideographs and the Korean syllabary were introduced into Japan.

Towards the end of the prehistoric period, legend begins to crystallise into history. There is definite evidence of the existence of an imperial court in the province of Yamato, the site of the capital changing with each reign. Relations with Korea, in particular with the court of Kudara, one of three kingdoms of that peninsula, appear to have been frequent and cordial; and it was from this source that the Buddhist faith and the first Buddhist images reached Japan.

Asuka Period (548—645)

Dates begin to be comparatively reliable and there seems no reason to dispute the year 538 as marking the arrival of the first missionaries. They were welcomed at the court of Yamato and, in spite of some persecution instigated by the influential Mononobe family, the rival Soga clan soon triumphed and Buddhism became firmly established. Monks, artists and artisans were encouraged to immigrate from Korea and China; they found eager and talented pupils.

At the turn of the century emerges that uncommon phenomenon, a man of peace who was also a man of destiny. Prince Shōtoku became regent for his aunt, Empress Suiko, in 593, at the age of twenty-one. A devout Buddhist, he not only fostered relations with China by sending an embassy there; he imported Chinese administrative techniques, a code of laws and a calendar. He organised education, encouraged religion and art. The Hōryuji temple at Nara is but one visible monument of this enlightened prince; his cultural influence was incalculable and it still endures. For twelve centuries no word was written, no picture painted, no metal wrought, that did not owe something to Shōtoku Taishi. He died in 623; by that time there were forty-six Buddhist temples in Japan, with all that implies in art and learning. The seed imported from China had taken firm root. The style was naturally enough that of the Wei and Sui Dynasties; but it soon acquired characteristics of its own. A cultural spring, comparable to that which blossomed in France in the twelfth century under the impulsion of Abbot Suger, overspread Yamato and the adjacent provinces. Bronze statues were cast with a technical perfection that soon surpassed their Chinese prototypes. Large wooden statues were carved, many of which have happily been preserved; and these

8

are the first works that show the development of individual Japanese styles — we must use the plural, for no fewer than three different schools are already distinguishable.

Styles of architecture, weapons and clothing are based on Chinese and Korean models; Chinese ideographs gradually supersede the Korean syllabary imported from Korea at an earlier stage. The nearest parallel in the West is the gradual diffusion of Greek culture in Rome. And it should be emphasised that although Japanese armies had already fought in Korea to support the allied kingdom of Kudara, the driving force was that of a religion of peace, swelling irresistibly eastward from India.

The court was still peripatetic, but Nara remained the artistic capital throughout the nine short reigns which followed that of Empress Suiko; in 710, a permanent imperial residence was established there.

The Nara Period (645—793)

The T'ang Dynasty had brought peace, order and prosperity to China; more frequent relations with the Chinese court, a two-way traffic of monks, scholars and craftsmen, could not fail to have a profound influence on the development of Japan. A stable capital was seen to be a necessity for a centralised administration and the imperial city of Nara closely followed the pattern of Ch'ang-an. Buddhism and Shintō (the indigenous animistic faith) both displayed a high degree of tolerance and adaptability, the first accepting the local Kami as manifestations of divinity and identifying them with those of the Indian creed. From this period no temples were exclusively Buddhist and few exclusively Shintō; yet the belief in a divine origin and a special dispensation for the oldest dynasty in the world has lived on into the middle of the twentieth century.

The Emperor Shōmu (724—48) enjoyed one of those long reigns which nearly always coincide with a period of stability and prosperity. By his command, a temple of the Kegon-shū sect was built in each province, all of them subordinated to the Tōdaiji temple at Nara, his *magnum opus*, the Monte Cassino of Japan. This edifice contained, and its successors still shelter, one of the most remarkable bronzes of all time, the *Nara Daibutsu*. But this statue was only the greatest of many that have survived in bronze, wood, clay and dry lacquer (textiles moulded and impregnated with lacquer on a mould which is subsequently withdrawn. This results in a very light image, suitable for carrying in procession).

The style has developed from the archaic formality of the Wei tradition and become more naturalistic. It has also acquired the restless energy of the T'ang style, the extreme of which is exemplified by the powerful figures of temple guardians, whose bulging muscles and ferocious expression may appear demoniac to European eyes, but whose latent menace is directed against the forces of evil.

9

Some painting of this period has survived, although the wonderful murals of Hōryuji Kondō were destroyed, after surviving 1200 years, by defective electrical wiring! To the piety and forethought of the Emperor Shōmu is due the oldest museum in the world, the Shōsōin at Nara, in which are housed the robes, instruments, weapons and household goods generally of the palace of his time. Many of them, particularly the musical instruments and work in precious metals, appear to be imports from China. But much of the lacquer is Japanese and the swords already foreshadow that perfect weapon whose fundamental characteristics were to remain unchanged for a thousand years. A number of masks, a distinctive highlight of Japanese art, have survived; they originated in the previous (Asuka) period and were used for the Gigaku, a ceremonial dance. Anyone who has ever seen a Japanese mask worn will testify to the uncanny characterisation it displays.

Gradually the riches bestowed on the temples came near to undermining the economy of the country; temple guards grew to be private armies of military monks; learned and industrious Benedictines were turning into powerful and truculent Templars. Kwammu Tennō (782—805) finally decided that Nara was too small to hold an emperor as well as an opulent theocracy, and in 794 he established his capital at Heiankyō, the present-day Kyōto.

The Heian Period (794—1184)

At the turn of the century, two new esoteric sects of Buddhism came to Japan. They introduced a new and formally prescribed iconography, covering every conceivable manifestation of divinity. Once again the style was that of contemporary Ch'ang-an, which had become somewhat exuberant and pretentious — we might almost describe it as Baroque. At the same time the first graven images of Shintō deities appear; they had hitherto been represented by symbols, such as the Mirror, Sword and Jewel of the Sacred Treasure, the crown jewels of a dynasty that extends back into the mists of prehistory.

Equally ancient and claiming descent from minor deities or early emperors were the *kuge* or court-nobles — an aristocracy whose main weakness was their lack of military tradition. Fastidiousness rather than any more discreditable instinct was probably responsible for the fact that few *kuge* cultivated the profession of arms. Scrambling through trackless forests in pursuit of repulsive savages — particularly when there is a sporting chance of being eaten by an elusive adversary after death by torture — has less appeal than a set-to with equals in the grim and gorgeous solemnity of a medieval battlefield. To equate the position with modern times, very few sons of rich men fell with Custer at the Little Big Horn.

But if few of the *kuge* were warriors, all of them were troubadours, and the Heian period was their golden age. Poetry, set down in calligraphy that is a poem in itself, was their pastime; dalliance, conducted according to the strictest rules of etiquette, their occupation.

In these circumstances it is natural that feminine influence grew; and the Fujiwara, the leading family of *kuge*, from one of whose five branches the emperor's consort was always chosen, gradually took advantage of the fact. By the end of the ninth century, a Fujiwara regent (Kwampaku) transacted all official business and regulated the succession; it is astounding that, among all the corrupting influences of a decadent court, this remarkable family could remain in power for 250 years.

Chinese influence remained preponderant for the first century of the Heian era; but the power and prestige of the great T'ang Dynasty gradually declined to its end in 910. The court of Heian found it impossible to maintain normal relations with a vast country in the throes of civil war. By this time, Japanese culture existed in its own right and began to develop along its own lines. Artists who had hitherto confined themselves to the decoration of temples began to produce pictures, on the panels of rooms, in albums or on scrolls for the delectation of the lay connoisseurs of the court, male and female. The first flowers of Japanese prose blossomed in the courtly romance of *Genji* by Lady Murasaki Shikibu and in the witty, catty and uninhibited reflexions of Sei Shōnagan in her 'Pillow Book'. The manuscripts were illustrated in the formal but fascinating style that came to be known as *Yamato-e*, with a lavish use of gold background, a naïve curiosity that removes the roofs of houses to disclose the happenings within, and an individuality that transcends the formal brush-strokes. From the tenth century, Buddhist painting, influenced by the doctrine propounded by the Jōdō sect, lays more emphasis on sweetness, gentleness and divine mercy whilst adhering to previous iconographic canons. At the same time the Japanese sense of fun and genius for caricature now manifests itself: in a few surviving scrolls animals carrying on human occupations are presented with a verve and sureness of line that any age and any country might envy. These were probably produced by monks in their lighter moments.

In sculpture, the monumental heaviness of the ninth-tenth centuries is succeeded by a gentle grace which, in the minor attendant angels, reminds one of the cheerful *putti* of the Italian Renaissance. The Verrocchio of this period is Jōchō. He introduced the technique of assembling figures from various pieces of wood instead of carving from a solid block, which minimises the risk of cracking as well as making the object lighter. A high level of achievement was attained in lacquer-work and textiles.

Something else was moving. At the beginning of the tenth century, the Japanese sword had taken the shape we know today. And while the court wrote poetry and played the incense game, someone had to maintain the perpetual vigilance that is the price of order as well as of freedom.

Younger sons of emperors and their descendants were given commands and estates in the outlying provinces. They administered these without interference from an unthinking, unthanking court to which they gave protection and formal homage. They levied and trained troops and built ships and learnt how to use them in the suppression of rebellion and piracy. The names of these clans were Minamoto and Taira: their clansmen were tough, disciplined and loyal; they were rivals for influence at court and a clash between them was bound to come.

It came in 1156. The *samurai*, with all his virtues and defects had been created. Japan entered a feudal period that was to last for 700 years.

The Hōgen War, beginning with a disputed succession to the throne in 1156, lasted three years and left the Taira clan in power. Taira no Kiyomori, a despot in the grand manner, built a magnificent palace at Fukuhara, organised an intelligence service and, having married his daughter to Emperor Takakura, raised his grandson to the throne at the age of two.

It is well to mention here that while usurpers of power forced the abdication of individual emperors, the dynasty itself has been challenged only once in Japanese history.

The surviving Minamoto had been restive for some time. Encouraged by the court, they rose in 1180. Kiyomori died in that year. The Taira were forced into the west and finally defeated in 1185.

The Kamakura Period (1185—1337)

Minamoto no Yoritomo, a cold-blooded and completely ruthless tyrant, having disposed of his younger brothers and their issue, caused himself to be proclaimed Shōgun and established his capital at Kamakura.

Loyalty, courage and austerity were the key-notes of the *samurai* code. If mercy was a minor consideration, we must remember that the knightly code of Europe was not always very strictly observed.

Such principles led naturally enough to austerity in art. Two other influences contributed to the development of Kamakura art; a conscious archaism, resulting from the restoration of the Nara temples, partially destroyed by the Taira, and the restraint and calm of Sung art — for relations with China had been renewed in the latter half of the twelfth century. Once again the influences were assimilated. We can see the transition from the gentle solemnity of Unkei's early style to the vivid but understanding realism of his later work. The Unkei-Tankei school was the last word in Japanese monumental sculpture. After the thirteenth century, few works exhibit any originality; with constant technical perfection, they are derived from those of an earlier period and have no greater merit than good Roman copies of Greek originals.

Buddhist painting has changed little. Some pictures are more naturalistic and present divinities and devotees against a background of familiar Japanese scenery. There are numbers of scrolls, some vivid representations of battles and lives of the saints in *Yamato-e* style; others, frankly caricatural, show the tortures endured by evil-livers after death or the everyday scene of human folly and suffering, not without a dash of *Schadenfreude*. Portraits are vigorous and unsparing. Sung influence is evident in the representation of nature, but few Kamakura pictures could be mistaken for Chinese as is possible in later periods.

One of the most noteworthy features of this period is the introduction into Japan of sophisticated ceramics. In 1223 the priest Dōgen took a Seto potter, later known as Tōshirō, to China with him; they stayed four years and Tōshirō made the most of his time with the Sung craftsmen. On his return to Japan, he succeeded in finding some suitable clay near and settled down to found a tradition.

He found his public at once in the Zen sect. Zen Buddhism (in Chinese, Ch'an) is unorthodox, individualistic, meditative, tinged with Taoism; it defies definition and will not be defined here. But if the author cannot define a tree, he can describe a leaf. Genuine Zen adepts seek inspiration in the perfection of small and humble things; in a flower, in an autumn leaf lying on the path, in firelight reflected on the dark glaze of a tea-bowl. Tea stimulates the mind; in taking tea, like Queen Anne, they took counsel. Of this simple, everyday pleasure the tea-ceremony was born. Its principles are as rigid as the cast-iron kettle in which the water boils; its rules are as elastic as the bamboo growing by the door of the modest hut where it takes place. The soldier leaves his great sword on the rack outside, to become, for a while, a monk and a poet. He exchanges the inexorable demands of war for the gentle discipline of nature. In so doing, he may become a better soldier and a happier man than the roisterer.

This ceremony has endured down to modern times, so the author may be excused for trespassing on the next period when he quotes from Okakura Kakuzo's *Ideals of the East*.

'Not to *use* the sword, but to *be* the sword — pure, serene, immovable, pointing ever to the Polar Star — was the ideal of the Ashikaga knight.'

These words are perhaps even more true of the period now under consideration. The power of the Minamoto died with Yoritomo; regents of the Hōjō family exercised authority in the name of infant Shōguns, shades of the Imperial Shadow. For a long time they wielded their power with justice and frugality and cultivated the military virtues.

The Mongol Yüan dynasty had conquered China by 1262. In 1268, Kublai Khan demanded the submission of Japan. The reply was an insult. Kublai Khan was not accustomed to such treatment, and in 1274, he sent an armada of 30,000 men to attack Kyūshū; about 17,000 returned to Korea.

The Mongol emperor waited until 1281 for his vengeance; then he launched 110,000 men against Japan. The Japanese forces concentrated too quickly to allow of effective deployment; the Tartars were confined to their beach-heads and after fifty days of bitter fighting, a 'Divine Wind' wrecked most of their fleet. It is estimated that this time, one-fifth of the broken force returned.

For another twenty years the Hōjō Shikken remained vigilant. But with a weak-minded and dissolute youth, this house in its turn relaxed its hold on Japanese history. And the Imperial Shadow came to life.

The Muromachi Period (1338—1573)

Gō-daigo Tennō came to the throne in 1319 at the age of 31. He was determined to restore the imperial power and secure the succession of his infant son. After two abortive plots, in which he was supported chiefly by the *kuge* and priests, he was exiled to an island and a usurper was enthroned.

A third plot was more successful. The Emperor escaped and Ashikaga Takauji, deserting the cause of the Hōjō, entered Kyōto with his troops, while Nitta Yoshisada took Kamakura. The emperor's cause had triumphed.

Unfortunately Gō-daigo was not a wise ruler, in spite of his determination; he rewarded the wrong people, and was unduly influenced by his favourites. Profiting by general discontent and attemps at rebellion, Takauji declared himself Shōgun in Kamakura in 1335.

The emperor was supported by a most noble figure, Kusunoki Masashige, the Montrose of Japan. Defeated as much by the emperor's courtly advisers as by the Ashikaga, Masashige's small force was overwhelmed at the Minatogawa, in 1336. Takauji installed another usurper and the emperor fled to the wild country of Yoshino. Nitta Yoshisada fought on, and died in battle in 1338. The so-called Southern Dynasty held out in Yoshino, defended by the heroic Kusunoki and Wada clans and assisted by dissensions in Kyōto until 1392, when Ashikaga Yoshimitsu, the third Shōgun, brought about a reconciliation of the two courts.

It was during this period that Zen Buddhism and the tea-ceremony came to fruition. The Ashikaga Shōguns favoured the Zen sect; Yoshimitsu sent embassies to the Ming court — Zen monks, who brought back many of the ink-paintings characteristic of Southern Sung art; and these began to have an effect on Japanese artists.

These pictures, which suggest more than they reveal, are meant for contemplation. A landscape is almost hidden behind a bank of cloud. Bamboo leaves shiver in the breeze and nothing, nothing distracts our attention from a single precious aspect of nature. A figure that is almost a caricature is intensely human in the framework of a few bold strokes. As a focal point for such contemplation, the *tokonoma*, the recess or niche, was created. It contains a picture, a vase with flowers and some other harmonious object, such as an incense-burner. Japanese rooms are not crowded as ours have been for many centuries. They display few of their possessions at any one time; and make certain that their impact on the eye and mind shall be effective.

This semi-monastic outlook has had a powerful influence on subsequent Japanese art. Shūbun, a priest who achieved great distinction in painting, was called to the Shōgunal court to found a school. Besides 'alcove paintings', he decorated the sliding panels of which Japanese rooms are formed and the large two- and six-fold screens, generally used in pairs in larger halls. Like all Japanese artists, he drifted away from the foreign canon; and in his pupils virtuosity tends to smother inspiration: the technique has become too perfect. His pupil Sesshū (1420—59) went to China to refresh himself at the fountainhead. After his return, he became a recluse, engrossed in his painting: his reputation stands very high.

Later, Kanō Masanobu (1453—90) borrowed some of the more solid technique of the *Yamato-e* school which continued to enjoy the patronage of the imperial court. These two elements were woven by his successors into the brilliant fabric of the Kano school, whose influence lives on today. The use of gold backgrounds and bright colours returned to popularity.

The luxury of the Ashikaga court was no doubt partly responsible for this. The influence of Ming painting was also felt, but is less important.

The Shōgun Yoshimitsu, who brought peace to Japan for a time, was both a statesman and patron of the arts. On leaving his sumptuous palace in the Muromachi quarter of Kyōto for the vigilant retirement so characteristic of Japan (1394), he built the magnificent Kinkaku-ji (Golden Pavilion). His grandson Yoshimasa was his equal in neither taste nor statesmanship. Civil wars raged, while the tea-ceremony luxuriated in a 'more-than-oriental-splendour' quite foreign to its principles. In an atmosphere of gold and tigerskins, sycophants and dancing-girls, he squandered millions, while in the provinces, potential rivals grew in power. After Yoshimasa the Ashikaga were no longer in effective control, and the stage was set for the civil wars of the sixteenth century.

In metalwork, a high degree of refinement was achieved — swords and their furniture, cast-iron kettles for the tea-ceremony, etc. The sword changes little, but the mountings become more ornate. Sword-guards, formerly a side-line of the armourer, unassuming and tasteful, begin to show scenes inlaid, first in brass, then in a variety of other metals.

Lacquer-work progresses in technical perfection and develops a greater freedom of design; miniature paintings of scenery, animals and persons take the place of regular and formal patterns.

Textiles languished, lacking the patronage of an impoverished court; the rich *daimio* obtained their fine brocades from China.

In the last hundred years of this period, tranquil intervals were few and loyalties uncertain. It is a story too long and complicated to be told here; as unhappy as the history of Aquitaine during the Hundred Years War. One event of major importance was the arrival of Portuguese ships with missionaries in 1542. Oda Nobunaga, a *daimio* whose power was then in the ascendant, favoured the Christians. By 1567, he was in effective control of the country. European influence is clearly discernible in the Japanese art of the latter half of the sixteenth century, particularly in lacquer and metalwork; some goods were exported to Europe, and Japanese envoys actually reached Rome and Madrid. But dissension set in amongst the missionaries; and the long, frail cord that bound Japan to Europe rotted. At the end of a generation it snapped.

The Momoyama Period (1568—1615)

This period, which takes its name from the palace built by Toyotomi Hideyoshi, was, in spite of intermittent warfare, favourable to the arts. Nobunaga only completed the subjugation of his enemies two years before his assassination in 1582. His general Hideyoshi, a man of obscure origins but of boundless energy, succeeded him. There is something of Napoleon in this man; in his genius, his restlessness and generous patronage of the arts. The power of the Buddhist monks having been broken, he discouraged, then persecuted the Christians, reluctant as any other tyrant to tolerate any influence on the conscience of his subjects which might conflict with his will. He twice invaded Korea; he was not very successful and died in 1598 during his second campaign. But he brought a fresh batch of Korean craftsmen back to Japan.

The Kanō school flourished, encouraged by his munificent orders for the decoration of palaces and castles. The surviving paintings of Kanō Eitoku give us some idea of the golden background against which these warriors moved. Great castles of cyclopean masonry were built, in imitation of medieval European practice, although the architectural effect was very different.

Hideyoshi carried his admiration of the tea-ceremony to extremes. Sen no Rikyū became an arbiter of taste whose influence endures to this day. But he chanced to offend his master and was condemned to die.

The manufacture of porcelain was introduced at Arita by the Korea potters brought back by Hideyoshi. Freshness of inspiration in pottery as well is evident; the decoration of sword-furniture reached new heights. Lacquer of the finest quality and original inspiration was produced. Prosperity was such that the country — or rather its rulers — were able to afford the best.

After Hideyoshi's death, his right-hand man Tokugawa Ieyasu seized power after a short struggle with his rivals culminating in the bloody battle of Sekigahara in 1600.

The Edo Period (1615—1868)

Ieyasu received the title of Shōgun in 1603 (since the Tokugawa were a branch of the Minamoto, there was a precedent for this appointment). After his capture of Ōsaka Castle in 1615, no challenge to his authority was possible.

He founded a police state that was to last longer than any other in history. He established his capital at Yedo, the Tokyo of today; the *daimio* were compelled to spend part of the year there and to leave near relations in the capital for the other part. A vigilant secret police, a strict censorship, exclusion of foreigners and ruthless persecution of Christianity were among the features of the Tokugawa regime. The only narrow window looking on to the outer world was at Nagasaki, where the Chinese and Dutch were allowed to trade under strict and humiliating controls.

Nevertheless, order and peace of a sort prevailed. Prosperity followed; and for the first time the artisan and commercial classes began to count for something — swordsmiths as well as artists had always occupied a special position. A climate favourable to a wide-spread dissemination of artistic appreciation was created; in this climate fine craftsmanship flourished and several new art-forms arose. Medicine-cases known as *inro* were made in the best taste and with superb technique; *netsuke*, the wooden or ivory toggles by which *inro* were suspended from the belt, became miniature works of art. Most of the sculpture of this period is repetitive, although outstanding specimens are found.

In painting, the Kanō school continued to dominate the scene but lost the fire of originality. The versatile Ōgata brothers Kōrin and Kenzan, inspired by Honami Kōetsu, produced some very striking work in pottery and lacquer as well as painting. The most noticeable feature of the latter half of the seventeenth century is the emergence of the colour print.

Sword furniture became more and more elaborate in technique. Extremely fine bronzes were cast, many of them in the Chinese manner. European influence is noticeable, particularly in the colour prints. Porcelain and pottery achieved great technical perfection; we observe a gradual decline in taste due to the demands of the European market.

After the Restoration of 1868, Japanese art began to influence Europe, greatly to the advantage of the latter; the converse does not, unfortunately, hold good. Cheap rubbish, catering for the worst taste, was exported in masses. But Japanese standards of taste have been maintained, especially among the most humble, to an astonishing degree, despite the impact of Western influences and an industrial revolution.

Sculpture

Sculpture, if not the earliest form of art, is without doubt the most enduring and, together with weapons, the most expressive of the personality of a people.

Unfortunately, the Japanese islands are poor in suitable stone, and any wooden sculpture that may have originated in prehistoric times has perished owing to the damp climate. We are left with the pottery *Jomon* and *haniwa* figures. The former are believed to have originated in a fertility cult; the earliest ones are crudely naturalistic. Those of later date are conventionalised and incised to indicate clothing. The duration of this period is disputed but it is not likely to cover less than a millennium and ends approximately with the Christian era.

Passing over the Yayoi period, when no sculpture has yet been positively identified, we come to the *haniwa*.

These figures in fired pottery on tubular bases are believed to originate about the third century A.D. They represent humans, saddle-horses, monkeys, dogs, etc. Their happy spontaneity must arouse regret for contemporary work that has perished.

One characteristic if minor form of art deserves a passing mention: the beads known as *magatama* or curved jewels. In their simplest form, these resemble a bear's claw; some of the larger and more elaborate ones are more like a mammalian foetus. They are made of various kinds of stone and are undoubtedly of magical significance, but whether the fertility theme or the religious awe accorded to the bear by many early cultures is the dominant factor, it is impossible to say.

With the introduction of Buddhism in the sixth century, sculpture finds its feet (and very big ones they are!); and the course of Japanese art is set for the next 1200 years. The images of the Buddha, mostly in gilt bronze, came from Kudara. They and their nearly contemporary Japanese successors, are based upon Indian art of the fourth century, modified by Chinese influences. The work of the Korean and Chinese artists settled in Japan is not distinguishable from that of their Japanese pupils. The first sculptor we known by name was Tōri Busshi, the grandson of a Chinese immigrant, who produced the magnificent gilt bronze Triad of Hōryuji in 623. In the work of his school, as in that of his predecessors, the influence of Northern Wei art (cf. the

Lung-Men caves) is very pronounced; in the case of some small bronzes, it would be hard to say whether they are Chinese or Japanese. The size of the feet is exaggerated in the interests of stability, that of the head for iconographic emphasis. The features and drapery are gracious in spite of their rigid formality and have affinities with archaic Greek statues. These bronzes as well as wooden figures have the same sense of latent life which inspired Flecker to write:

> And once I touched a broken girl
> And knew that marble bled.

The *mandara*, or flaming aureoles, of these statues set them off to perfection. They are usually studded with miniature Bodhisattvas.

Besides Amida, the historic Buddha, the favourite subjects are Kannon (Avalokitesvara) and Miroku (Maitreya, the coming Buddha). The Miroku shown here (Plate 2) is probably one of the 112 recorded at the Hōryuji Temple at Nara in the inventory of 1078, of which seventy-two are known still to be in Japan; much Buddhist art of major importance left the country in the 1880's, when official support had been withdrawn from Buddhism and the Government was concerned with other things. It is twelve inches high and a very heavy casting in almost pure copper.

A striking fact is that the bronze-founders managed to do such remarkable work with irregular alloys, never twice the same, and improbable methods; this applies to later periods as well.

While the bronzes are derived from the Chinese, the contemporary wooden statues are very much closer to the Indian idiom. The reason for this is a matter for speculation. At all events, in spite of obvious foreign influence, they are clearly Japanese and nothing else. For the first time we perceive that inherent *feeling* for material which has characterised the craftsmen of Japan for the best part of two millennia. The grain of the wood is chosen to follow selected lines of the subject.

The influence of T'ang art on the Japanese in the Nara period was rapid and pronounced. Bronzes and the surviving wooden statues are very close to their Chinese prototypes and the best are in no way inferior. The magnificent bronze Bodhisattvas of the Yakushiji Temple, Nara, are among the finest examples (Plate 3). Archaic stiffness has gone; they cannot be called naturalistic although the trend is in that direction. They have a transcendent solemnity that equals where it does not surpass the best art of the Gupta period in India. And it is no overstatement to say that nothing of their kind as fine as the Gigaku and Bugaku masks mentioned in the Introduction have ever been produced in any country. Another feature of T'ang sculpture that has been transplanted is the fierce temple guardians (Plate 5).

To the European critic at least, the sculpture of the early Heian period appears less admirable. The importation of two new sects of esoteric Buddhism resulted in an intense concentration on a formal iconography that recalls the worst features of Alexandrian and Indian art minus their light-heartedness. The supernatural has become a fat, stylised superlative of the sensuous, an earnest, orientalised rococo. It corresponds with a debasing of the bright coin of Buddhism; and it is a relief to turn to the rare statues of Shintō deities which now occur (they were previously represented by such objects as a sword or mirror) and to portraiture. Once again, the Graeco- and Romano-Egyptian parallel imposes itself. Beauty is truth, even when truth takes the form of grim, ascetic old hunkses.

In the latter part of the Heian period, the Nara influence is once more felt, with the school of Jōchō (c. 1057); in his work, divinity ceases to be a distorted concept of humanity and returns to the simpler idealism that pervades Japanese art in subsequent centuries. A new technique was also established; statues were assembled from selected pieces of wood, making them lighter in weight and less liable to distortion and cracking.

The Kamakura period is inaugurated by Unkei, a genius of the greatest versatility. His earlier work shows the influence both of the Nara period and of the passionless, balanced sculpture of Sung China; his ferocious temple guardians are completely Oriental and express the spirit of a grim period of wars, whereas his portraits of Buddhist priests — for portraits they are, although they depict legendary characters — would not seem out of place in Florence, Paris or Augsburg. The benevolent, care-worn expression and the fall of the draperies is, quite simply, perfect.

Nec plus ultra: almost the last original word was spoken in the thirteenth century. After that, Japanese sculptors had magnificent examples to copy. The carvers of masks (among whom the Deme family is outstanding) produced lively, uncanny characterisation well into the nineteenth century. Some later sculptors have given us perceptive impressions of animals and humorous versions of Daruma. For the rest, they were content to follow humbly (and very competently) in the steps of superb predecessors.

Inspiration, however, found a refuge in small things, to wit, *netsuke*. About the end of the sixteenth century, men began to carry *inro*. These were fastened through the obi (sash) by small toggles, which very soon began to take the form of animals or persons. Some of the earliest are Chinese ivory seals in the form of *kylins* or *shishi;* before the seventeenth century had run half its course, every available material and subject had been exploited in the manufacture of these fascinating objects. History, imagination and humour combined to serve a high degree of craftsmanship. Vast quantities exist and are prized by many collectors; yet it is hard to find a specimen made before 1850 that is not in excellent taste. The majority are carved in wood, ivory or stag-horn; they are frequently signed, and a considerable body of literature in European languages is devoted exclusively to them. The simplest ones are generally the most appealing — small birds, fat puppies, contemplative horses, Nō masks.

If the Yedo period had produced nothing except the *netsuke*, this would still form no mean artistic heritage.

Painting

The history of Japanese painting must inevitably start with the Tamamushi shrine (Plate 10) in the Hōryuji Temple at Nara, together with the wall-painting destroyed by fire in 1949 but fortunately recorded with great accuracy (Plates 12, 13).

The former belongs, strictly speaking, under the heading of lacquer, for that is the medium; but its artistic and documentary importance impose its classification as a painting. It was made probably about the year 620, represents scenes in the lives of Buddha, and is in the style of the Chinese Wei Dynasty. Here, as in sculpture, continental influences were preponderant.

The murals of the Kondō were painted, probably, a century later. They have been described as the finest achievement of Mahayana Buddhist art and few will quarrel with that statement. Indian inspiration is obvious; it seems improbable though not impossible that the influence was direct instead of passing first through northern China. The technique used has not been completely elucidated.

Among the few survivals from the Nara period, we should mention the well-known Kichijōten of the Yakushiji in which the Chinese influence is very marked and the E-Ingakyō, an illustrated sutra. The monk who painted it took less pains than a contemporary Benedictine would have devoted to a missal, but it is full of naïve vigour; the purpose and feeling are similar.

Before going any further some reference must be made to materials and technique. Japanese and Chinese pictures are normally painted either on silk or on paper made from the bark of the mulberry tree. The prepared surface is placed, not on an easel, but flat on the floor, and the artist works kneeling. Writing is done in the same way and there is a greater affinity between writing and painting than in Europe. The decorative quality of Chinese ideographs is obvious and calligraphy is highly prized. The signature, seals, poems and appreciations often appended to a painting form a part of the composition, and outstanding examples of calligraphy are mounted for their own sake. It is a case of 'any story makes a picture'.

For both purposes, brushes of various calibres and Indian ink are used. The blocks of ink are rubbed with water on a flat abrasive stone, generally a shale, with a recess at one end to catch the prepared ink. In many cases, a picture is entirely in black and white, with the subtle gradations which masterly brush-work makes possible. Certainty and purity of line are achieved by years of painstaking practice. This virtue, like most others, has its drawbacks: it trains admirable copyists. On the other hand, many fine pictures would never have survived but for the copyists; and in the hands of a master practice achieves perfection indeed.

Naïve, untrained genius we can accept; but true genius is rarely slipshod. There may be substitutes for a conscience in social life: there are none in art.

Colour is then applied — normally an opaque gouache, and no indication of shadows (the Hōryuji murals are an exception). But the grouping of colours forms a part of the composition. Gold and silver are used with great effect, sometimes in details and sometimes as a ground. The latter technique is a characteristic of the *Yamato-e* school of painting which begins in the Heian period.

The Buddhist paintings of the earlier Heian period are in the style of T'ang China and much affected by the esoteric canons of the Tendai and Shingon sects. As in sculpture, the over-emphasis, distortion and portentousness of this style, while still esteemed by Japanese critics, is less agreeable to the European eye than the more gracious paintings inspired by the teachings of the Amida sect in the latter half of the period. In these we revert to the simplicity and gentleness of the Nara period; both sect and style were favoured at the court. Painting is now decorated with cut gold leaf which, pleasing in itself, tends to distract the eye from the major features of the composition. Landscapes in the Chinese manner for the houses of the nobility, on partitions and screens, now evolve to a presentation of Japanese scenery in the *Yamato-e* or Japanese style. The Kitanō Tenjin Engi (relating the story of the foundation of the Kitanō Tenjin shrine) is one of the best examples of the scrolls of this period where the whole story was told in pictures without any interpolation of text. The Genji Monogatari, many copies of which must have been made, is another. The conventional rendering of details does not detract from the liveliness of the whole.

Toba Sōjō, a Buddhist abbot, seems to have been the originator of the humorous scrolls referred to in the Introduction. The influence of his school stretches on into the Kamakura period. The verve — occasionally coarse and rather bitter — of these drawings is the form of light relief one might expect of an age in which courage and austerity occupy the foreground of the picture.

In the Kamakura period the range of painting for the laity increases; stories, battles, legends, portraits and landscapes depict almost exclusively Japanese subjects in an unmistakeably Japanese style although Sung influence is discernible. Some very remarkable portraits have survived.

In the Muromachi period the influence of Zen Buddhism becomes predominant, as does Chinese influence on painting. It is not the rich luxuriance of the Ming style, but the gentle, misty nostalgia of the 'Southern' Sung school, which being at that time less esteemed in China, permitted the accumulation of a number of masterpieces in Japan. And these, with an infusion of native genius, were responsible for the rise of the Kanō School.

Kanō Masanobu was eclipsed by his son Motonobu, who still remained fairly close to the Chinese style of ink-painting. But Shūbun, his son Geiami and grandson Sōami and his pupil Sesshū are closer to the Sung feeling.

At the same time, the Tosa school emerges from the *Yamato-e*. Owing no doubt to its decorative qualities, it managed to survive, and even to influence, its rival, as is seen in the work of Motonobu and his illustrious grandson Eitoku. This brings us to the Momoyama period, dominated by the Kanō school with a few independent exceptions such as Hasegawa Tōhaku and Sōtatsu.

The Yedo period saw the rise of the Ukiyoe school (see *Prints*). Tanyū and Tsunenobu were among the most distinguished Kanō artists. The greatest follower of Sōtatsu was the vigorous and versatile Ōgata Kōrin. The influence of Chinese refugees settled in Nagasaki after 1644 was responsible for the Bunjinga or Scholars' school, whose aggressive individualism is perhaps most happy in bold impressionistic sketches. At its best, European influence could inspire Maruyama Okyō to a harmonious synthesis in the middle of the eighteenth century; at its worst, in the early Meiji period, it sometimes produced a combination suggesting sardines and strawberries.

Metalwork

The use of metals was introduced to Japan in the Yayoi period, probably in two distinct phases: a Bronze Age, characterised by burial in round barrows, in which bronze swords have been found, but no iron. In the later phase, when interment in vast keyhole-shaped dolmens begins, iron and bronze are found together, the latter being used for mirrors, sword-mounts and long bells called *dotaku*, the use of which is unknown. All this early metalwork follows continental types and must include some imports. Even the *dotaku*, which are characteristically Japanese, have an affinity with early Chinese bells.

Soon, definite Japanese types are found, some with a rather barbaric exuberance, such as little bells on the edge of mirrors. But as we climb over the rim of legend and look out on the landscape of history, such excrescences disappear and we see Japanese art appropriating the best and adapting it to a national idiom.

Casting in bronze was the first great achievement and has been mentioned in the Introduction and under the subject of sculpture. At the same time as figures, bells, lanterns, etc., many of them with fine and generous gilding were made; many have only survived with the gilt scraped off in some extremity of need or vandalism. But the temples of Nara are still rich in fine metalwork of the Asuka and Nara periods.

To turn for a moment to iron, it is in the Nara period and probably about 700 that the Japanese sword begins to assume its historic shape, the earliest smith named being the legendary Amakuni. The swords of Emperor Shōmu in the Shōsōin have already all the outstanding features except the curve. But it is not until about 900, with the smith Yasutsuna, that the great hawk-like blades emerge in all their splendour.

Apart from the legendary esoteric significance of the sword, the labour and expense involved in the forging of these superbly functional objects naturally led to their being cherished as the greatest treasures of their owner; the monetary value eventually placed upon the best of them sometimes ran into thousands of pounds. They were given individual names, such as 'Little Crow' or 'Knee-cutter'; in the sixteenth century the gift of a famous sword became equivalent to that of a fief.

Few Japanese swords were forged exclusively of steel, the core of the blade being normally welded into a matrix of softer iron in order to minimise the risk of breaking. The bulk of the blade was covered with clay for tempering; the exposed edge took a harder temper when quenched. The pattern or *yakiba* along the edge, together with the graining of the metal caused by repeated folding, are points to which the expert looks when judging a blade. This weapon is designed primarily for cutting, and thrusts were rare.

It has been said that if a European and a Japanese, both expert fencers, were opposed with their respective weapons, *both* would certainly be killed!

Swords were often signed, sometimes dated (over 12,000 smiths have been recorded), and were made in various lengths, from great two-handers to dirks a few inches long. The *samurai* always wore two, long and short.

The attempted invasions gave a great impetus to the manufacture of swords. By common consent Masamune of Sagami (1264—1343) is considered the greatest smith that ever lived, and blades by his ten best pupils are rated almost as highly as his. Unlike the European knight, the *samurai* was also an archer. The Japanese bow is one-and-half times the height of the owner and is held below the centre. The three-foot arrows are tipped with steel heads of various shapes, mainly armour-piercing, but some of beautiful and intricate design (Plate 27).

The armour is designed primarily as protection against arrows and consists mainly of lacquered steel lames loosely held together by silk cord, the sleeves being of mail. It lacks the sculptural quality of European armour. The usual helmet is a bowl consisting of a number of rivetted plates (sixty-four is by no means uncommon); it is supplemented by a separate mask with gorget and has a neck-guard, the size and angle of which varied according to the prevailing fashion.

The early sword-guards (with the exception of those for ceremonial mounts) were made by armourers, among whom the Miochin family is pre-eminent over twenty-seven generations, beginning in the twelfth century. This family also produced master-pieces of forged iron for civilian use and ornament until modern times.

With great regret it must be admitted that the accurate dating of pierced sword-guards earlier than the first half of the fifteenth century is at present impossible. Some armourer's guards may be attributed to the thirteenth century — but with a hundred years' room on either side. They did not at that time enjoy the esteem accorded to later and more elaborate productions and many must have been scrapped. With the beginning of inlay in soft metals on iron in the fifteenth century, we are on firmer ground. Brass was used at first, then damascening in gold or silver, then the whole gamut of pictorial inlay.

A word must be said of cast iron. Nothing noteworthy in this material was produced until the fifteenth century, when kettles of great beauty and perfection were cast for use in the tea ceremony; the technique persists well into modern times.

To return to the softer metals — it is clear that the casting of bronze was mastered in prehistoric times and reached perfection in the Nara period. The bell of Tōdaiji weighs forty-nine tons and was cast in 732; the great Buddha of the same temple, dedicated in 756, is fifty-three feet high and was cast in stages. The bell is only four tons lighter than the largest one in China, which was cast in 1406. And although many of the smaller pieces of gilded and inlaid metalwork in the Shōsōin appear to be Chinese, there are enough chased and gilt boxes, lanterns and other ornaments to confirm the artistry and skill of the Japanese craftsmen of the Nara and Heian periods.

The noteworthy developments of the Kamakura period were in the field of sculpture and in the adornment of armour. Not until the Muromachi period do we find much that is new in fine sword furniture.

Then, about the same time as inlays in soft metal begin to appear on iron sword-guards, the beginnings of the Gōtō school are recorded with Gōtō Yujō, who worked for the Shōgun Yoshimasa. This school was the forerunner of the host of artists who produced decorative soft metal fittings for swords.

These consist of the *kashira* or pommel, the *menuki* or grip ornaments, the *fuchi* or collar, the *tsuba* or guard, the *kodzuka* or hilt of the general purpose knife, the *kōgai*, a stylus, the *kurikata* or fastening-boss and the *kojiri* or chape. They are adorned with formal patterns, animals, flowers, historic or legendary scenes, often derived from paintings, in gold, silver and various alloys that give a wide range of colour. Among the finest achievements of the mount-makers is the clever use of *shakudo*, a copper alloy with traces of gold, to which a blue-black patina was imparted by a secret process.

The ground of these exquisite miniature pictures is sometimes flat, sometimes 'fish-roe' punched. For sheer technical virtuosity they are unrivalled in any country. Cellini would have been proud to acknowledge anything as good as a set of sword-mounts by one of the Japanese masters. The technique continues to within living memory, through many schools, and embraces articles of household and personal use, such as pouch-clasps. It was perhaps inevitable that, catering for more flamboyant tastes, some inlaid work from the eighteenth century on tended to be smothered with intricate detail. But the best remained as good as ever.

Up to the sixteenth century bronze incense burners and flower vases in the Chinese manner were made largely for religious use. After that time, household bronzes in the Ming style began to be cast for the laity. They soon acquired a Japanese accent, and in spite of some aberrations of taste, very fine ones have been produced down to the present day.

Lacquer and Textiles

We have of late become accustomed to substances known as plastics, which will protect anything against almost anything else. The earliest of these substances is quite simply the juice of the lacquer tree, a native of south-east Asia. The fact that it polymerises in contact with air to form a translucent, insoluble mass was discovered very early in China, certainly by the seventh century B.C. The tree is believed to have been introduced into Japan in the third century A.D.; its products were certainly known in the sixth and lacquer ware had reached a high degree of perfection by the eighth. As usual, most of the early examples are in the Shōsōin at Nara. Scholars are not agreed as to which of them are Japanese and we will not go further than to say that there seems no reason why a people who could cast a fifty-three foot bronze statue should be unable to decorate a wooden box.

These early lacquers are in the style of T'ang China; some are on leather, on metal mirrors or on material. Metal is as bad a foundation for lacquer as any owing to its high coefficient of expansion and its liability to surface oxidation. The most suitable technique and the most generally employed is to paint the *urushi* (filtered lacquer-tree sap) on to wood tightly covered with silk or other material. A number of coats is used, each of which is allowed to dry in a damp chamber. Colour is obtained by adding various substances, e.g. digested iron filings for black, cinnabar for red, etc. The ground is often sprinkled with gold- bronze- or tin-dust *(nashiji)*, the final coat being transparent.

The thirty processes necessary to produce fine lacquer and their elaborate terminology cannot be dealt with in detail. The reader should remember four words: *roiro*, black lacquer, *nashiji*, metal-sprinkled ground, *makie*, decoration in relief with metal inlay, etc. and *togidashi*, flat decoration under a polished surface.

Pearl-shell inlay enjoyed great popularity in early times, and again from the late sixteenth century to the present. The effect can be superb in the hands of a first-class artist.

It is hard to find a use to which lacquer has not been put, and its convenience probably inhibited the production of fine ceramics until a fairly late period; for at the same time as the finer qualities much 'utility lacquer' must have been made which has not survived.

The earliest known piece of lacquer in Japan is the famous Tamamushi shrine, which has been dealt with under *Painting;* another early piece is a cupboard of about 680 A.D. in the Shōsōin; it is of little technical or artistic interest. But the lacquer of the Nara period in the same storehouse or museum is of the highest quality; the designs are generally formal, inlaid in silver, gold and pearl-shell in the T'ang style. Tortoise-shell has also been used in combination with pearl-shell, gold and lacquer on the backs of mirrors; the result has unfortunately not been durable. The earliest gold lacquer known is on the scabbard of Shōmu Tennō's sword.

In the Heian period, gold lacquer makes further progress, and red cinnabar lacquer appears. More objects for lay use have been preserved, and a Japanese style develops. No work can definitely be ascribed to the ninth century; the scripture-box formerly in the Ninnaji temple near Kyōto, decorated with angels and conventional flowers in gold and silver lacquer must have been made about 920. The base is not wood but cloth (the 'dry lacquer' technique). The dates of a few other pieces before 1200 are firmly established, such as the superb 'wheels in waves' casket in the Imperial Collection. By this period Japanese lacquer was not only emancipated from Chinese styles but had reached a technical perfection that was never to be surpassed.

The austerity of style characteristic of the Kamakura period was less apparent in lacquer than in any other medium. New techniques evolved and we have gold-ground *(kinji)* boxes, where the soft gleam of the gold is sometimes lit up by flashes of irridescent pearl-shell. A variety where successive uneven layers of red and black lacquer were rubbed through to make a cloudy pattern enjoyed a certain popularity. The love of nature characteristic of Japanese art in most of its phases is now dominant.

To Japanese critics, the Muromachi period is the golden age of lacquer; for some others, its technical perfection overlays artistic inspiration. Be that as it may, what one expects to find on a tray or writing-box is a pattern or a pleasant and evocative miniature, not a breath-taking work of art. Dimension itself is a factor in aesthetics. Enlarge a Nicholas Hilliard miniature, it will never be a great painting. Reduce the *Rout of San Romano* to the dimensions of a snuff-box; it is a pretty thing but no longer inspiring.

And so the formal patterns on lacquer are pleasing and dignified. Attempts to produce a *Yamato-e* subject or a landscape in the Southern Sung style on a writing box . . . are fine miniatures.

And in the last unhappy century of this period, the lacquer industry shared the fate of Kyōto, burnt and sacked; even its technique was in eclipse until Hideyoshi's time. Then with returning prosperity and increased stability, lacquerers found a market for fine objects and catered for it in their own way. Such was their enthusiasm that their pictures overflowed the edges of the boxes and continued down the sides. What remained on the top was always a balanced composition. Freshness of inspiration was however offset by a certain inferiority in the quality of the lacquer. A technical tradition that has died is often hard to revive; and this was a slapdash age. Pearl-shell inlay returned to favour, lead or pewter were also used and their dull surface makes a pleasing foil for the high-polished *roiro* and gleaming gold. Chests with formal patterns were produced to European order and, in these, pearl-shell predominates.

The work of a versatile genius, Hōnami Kōetsu, sword-expert, painter, lacquerer and potter, takes us well into Edo period. He and his followers Kōrin and Kenzan produced bold and imaginative work which is as much appreciated — and imitated — today at it was in the seventeenth century.

In the Edo period, lacquer once more attains a high degree of technical perfection and follows many styles. The best artists were responsible for designs carried out by unsurpassed craftsmen. A new field for this material was found in the *inro* or medicine-case — delightful objects which were produced in tens of thousands, right up to the end of the nineteenth century. In them we find the controlled exuberence of a people who wore no jewellery and of a caste whose clothing was subdued in colour.

Most of the lacquer produced in this period, if not high art, was at least in excellent taste; we cannot follow it in detail. Even in Japan, of course, vulgarity is to be found if we look for it — among those of whom we might expect it; the average standard of taste is higher than in any other country.

In the nineteenth century rich gold lacquer appears, sometimes combined with silver trimmings and inlaid with coral, ivory and pearl-shell etc. It is very nice for those who like it.

Good lacquer should be protected from dust and sunlight, and rubbed very gently, if at all. No soap or alkali, above all, ammonia, should be used; a little sweet oil and water does no harm.

Textiles

While it is probable that some form of textiles were used in Japan as far back as the Stone Age, nothing prior to the Asuka period has survived. The clothing on the *haniwa* figures appears to be similar to that of contemporary China. The earliest known textile fragment is an embroidered banner commemorating Shōtoku Taishi; it is extremely lively and pleasing, the work is good and the colour has remained fresh. This is embroidery; but a number of brocades and damask fragments exist. They are very fine, and it is known that such silks were even exported to China at the end of the seventh century. 'Batik' technique and stencilling were also practised.

Most of these textiles are of Sassanian inspiration, *via* China, which persisted, alongside the gradual development of a Japanese style during the Heian era, until the fourteenth century. The surviving fragments are, as usual, religious vestments; some fragments of court robes may have intruded in *kesa*, patchwork humeral veils of Buddhist priests. These robes, voluminous and stiff, had become very different from Chinese costume. Obviously the luxurious court of Heian demanded the finest quality; but no technical innovations are apparent.

The austerity of the Kamakura period expresses itself in simplification and sobriety of garments as well as in textiles of inferior quality. Chinese brocades were now highly prized and scraps used for the mounting of Kakemono and as bags for tea-jars.

During the Muromachi period, the same trend continues. Except for ceremonial occasions, stiff voluminous robes are superseded by the *kōsode*, the ancestor of the kimono. During the latter half of this era and in the Momoyama period, the increasing interest in Nō plays led to the production of gorgeous robes for the drama. Textiles imported from Java, India and even Europe became popular and had considerable influence on design. In Hideyoshi's time a number of Chinese weavers who were working in Sakai (Izumi) were resettled in the Nishijin quarter of Kyōto, where their influence endures today.

Techniques of infinite elaboration were mastered and foreign influences harmoniously digested. Except under the baneful influence of foreign vulgarity, Japanese textiles have never looked back since that time.

Ceramics

In the tombs of the Yayoi and Dolmen periods, we find grey wheel-thrown pottery, sometimes hard enough to display a natural glaze and quite different from the *haniwa* surrounding the dolmens. Many articles closely resemble similar finds in Korea; cups, bowls and jars are perched on conical stands pierced with square or triangular holes. Some vases blossom out into smaller vases emerging from the shoulder of the parent pot or into figures of men and animals, a style well-known in the Mediterranean. Others have rounded bottoms and are marked with a mat-pattern. Fertility of invention and sense of form are a long way ahead of technique; and it is hardly safe to identify any sophisticated glazed pottery in Japan before the thirteenth century. Numerous kilns are recorded; many specimens exist, simple grey bowls and jars with no trace of glaze, coiled jars finished on the wheel, with crude glazing, none of which can be definitely located either in time or space. It is an exasperating gap, which leads one to assume that lacquer was extensively used at court and that no effort was made to improve pottery. The pottery found in the Shōsōin with green and brown glazes and one or two similar finds from the provinces are commonly considered to have been imported from China, while certain Japanese scholars of the present day maintain that some were produced in Japan. Further evidence would be welcome.

Katō Shirozaemon, a potter whose name is generally abbreviated to Tōshirō, is said to have gone to China in 1223; after a few years, he returned, having learnt some Chinese techniques and started a kiln at Seto — a site which subsequently became so famous that pottery objects are often called *Seto-mono*. A vast number of kiln sites in this area have been investigated and have yielded fragments glazed in brown, yellow and black: high-fired pottery which, though not equal to contemporary Chinese products, show that definite progress had been made.

Without going into details of the products attributed to Tōshirō, his son and grandson, it will suffice to say that early in the Kamakura period, the Zen sect and the tea-cult were beginning to make their mark. The superb achievements of the Sung potters were highly esteemed in Japan, particularly Chien Yao. In course of time, they were satisfactorily imitated at Seto.

One can hardly do better than to quote Otto Kümmel: 'The characteristics of Japanese pottery, deserving of this name in a special sense, do not lie on the surface; they do not manifest themselves in glistening material and sumptuous decoration or in that virtuosity of technique most likely to attract the attention of a European. To recognise them requires calm contemplation and a measure of devotion without which no aesthetic enjoyment is possible but which today, as indeed at any period, is a capacity possessed by few . . . Purely decorative utensils, things inadequate to their purpose which are ashamed of being utensils, were never made in Japanese pottery. And here Japanese *export* pottery (which is what most Europeans understand by the term) stands condemned. It was indeed made by Japanese but not for themselves and so belongs to Japanese art only in a topographical sense, or as Brinkley so truly says: "it is nothing more than a Japanese estimate of our own bad taste".'*

From the Middle Ages it is chiefly the treasured implements of the tea ceremony that have survived: the *cha-ire* (caddy), *cha-wan* (tea-bowl), *kōro* (incense-burner), *mizu-zashi* (water-jar). Many of these show cracks or chips, beautifully repaired with lacquer. In later times, when the simplicity of the tea ceremony had become rather laboured, a repair on one of the implements became a point in its favour; and it must be confessed that the threads of gold lacquer on the rugged surface of an old *cha-wan* have great charm. Certain ancillary equipment must be mentioned: the slender caddy-spoon of bamboo or ivory, the bamboo flower-vases, which were often made by the *cha-jin* (connoisseurs) themselves and require a truly contemplative eye to appreciate their simple and perfect line. The bamboo whisk and ladle are expendables and need not detain us. *Cha-wan* and *cha-ire* of outstanding merit were heirlooms only one degree less precious than swords.

This being the case, how do they come to be obtainable at all? Not a Japanese, but an English poet gave the answer a century and a half ago:

> *When men change swords for ledgers and desert*
> *The students' bower for gold . . .*

No conspicuous progress was made during the Kamakura period, nor does the partiality of Yoshimasa for the tea ceremony seem to have broken any fresh ground in the field of pottery. But towards the end of the fifteenth century Shinō Sōshin, a famous tea-master, produced a grey 'candified' glaze with coarse crackling and sketchy underglaze decoration in blue and reddish brown. This attractive Shinō ware continues into modern times.

At the beginning of the Momoyama period, when political and economic conditions had begun to crystallise, the potters at Seto became very active, largely under the patronage of Lord Furuta Ōribe, a great tea-master, who inspired the production of

* Otto Kümmel, *Kunstgewerbe in Japan*, p. 101, Richard Carl Schmidt — Co., Berlin, 1922.

summarily decorated wares, with intermingling coloured overglazes. About the same time the manufacture of finely crackled yellowish Ki-Seto began. In the work of Furuta Ōribe's potters the beginnings of a certain conscious striving for the bizarre is discernible; a parasitic growth for which the tea-cult unfortunately offers favourable conditions. About this time some *cha-jin* began to mark their pieces.

Each stage of development, particularly during the sixteenth century, was assisted by fresh immigrations of Korean potters, and new kilns were started in a number of places, including Takatori, Karatsu, Hagi, Yatsushiro, Kyōto and Satsuma. Fawn-coloured, yellow and celadon glazes came into fashion, the latter with designs inlaid in white clay in the Korean manner. The pottery of Bizen seems to have been least affected by foreign influences; this is a very hard stone-ware, generally rust-brown but sometimes slate-grey *(Ao-Bizen)*.

Sen no Rikyū was perhaps the greatest of the tea-masters; his influence has been enduring and his precepts generally observed. It was in his time that Raku ware, originally produced by a Korean immigrant about 1550 and perfected by his son Chōjiro, became popular, doubly so because it could be potted and fired without much difficulty by amateurs. The paste of this ware is loose and friable, the glaze thick and treacly and crackled, generally black, grey or salmon-pink. The paste being a bad conductor of heat, Raku tea-bowls were especially popular. Most of them are hand-made, large and thick (Plate 38). Kōro and figurines were also produced. Hideyoshi esteemed Chojiro so highly that he presented him with a gold seal bearing the character *Raku*. And this trademark, with slight variations for each successive master, is still in use after fourteen generations.

The traditional forms and glazes of Seto continued and were brought to even greater perfection at Takatori in the next century. The influence of the tea-masters continued to grow, and the Tokugawa peace was most favourable to the arts. The most interesting personality of this period is Kōbori Mazakazu, Lord of Enshu. He himself maintained that his taste was inferior to that of Sen no Rikyū. That is arguable, but we must at least rate it higher than that of his old friend Ōribe.

Kōbori Enshu was the patron of several kilns, among them that of Shidoro.

In the second quarter of the seventeenth century Nonomura Ninsei began to work in Kyōto. He was a perfect master of various techniques, but is most famous for a fine cream or grey crackle decorated in brilliant overglaze enamels. His successors and imitators produced enormous quantities of this type, which finally degenerated into so-called 'Satsuma' in the finest technique. The best of it is charming, the worst overdecorated and quite appalling.

Kenzan, a younger brother of the artist Kōrin, was a potter of great taste and originality; the two often collaborated.

Porcelain came late to Japan. Blue and white is said to have been made by Shonzui, about 1500, with clay imported from China. The best European authorities maintain that he imported not the raw material but the finished article.

In 1605, vast deposits of china clay were discovered in Hizen and the manufacture of porcelain on a large scale began at Arita. The paste was at first greyer than that of Chinese porcelain, the shapes and designs simple and fresh. The European market pounced upon this ware; soon portentous jars, clotted with formal designs in red and gold, were being produced for those who knew no better. But towards the middle of the century Sakaida Kakiemon learnt from a Chinese refugee potter various technical secrets of which he made the best use for the home market. The perfect technique and delicate designs stand comparison with anything of this type ever produced in China. They were imitated very competently in Europe, notably at Meissen, and even in China. And the tradition, fortunately, did not die out.

The porcelain of Arita is commonly known to Europeans as Imari, the name of the harbour from which it was exported. Another factory not far from Arita produced porcelain of the finest quality ever made in Japan exclusively for the noble family of Nabeshima. The porcelain of Kutani, while cruder in paste and finish, is nevertheless very pleasing in the charm of its bold designs and the brilliance of the enamel colours.

It is not possible to deal with the innumerable factories working in Japan in the nineteenth century. Their best products were good, their worst almost as bad as those of industrial Germany at the same period.

Prints

Although black and white woodblock prints of Buddha were made as early as the eighth century, it is not until nearly a thousand years later that this technique started to develop into the Japanese prints so familiar to everyone.

Soon after 1600, books with illustrations began to appear, but no artists of talent worked on them. Presently the Ukiyoe or 'floating world' school of painting developed. Its origin has been attributed to one Iwasa Matahei but it should be considered rather as a spontaneous growth fostered by the prosperity and disciplined peace of the Tokugawa regime. A well-to-do merchant and artisan class of townsmen came into being whose tastes, while as frivolous as those of the Heian courtiers, were more earthy. They demanded pictures of everyday life; and among the more decorative features of that life were the Kabuki melodramas and the gorgeously apparelled courtesans of the Yoshiwara. And when wood-block engraving first engaged the attention of talented artists such as Hishigawa Moronobu and Okamura Masanobu, the beauties of the Yoshiwara came into their own.

Moronobu (d. 1694) never printed in colour. Some of his bold, lively work is hand-coloured but, on the whole, the pigments have not worn well. Masanobu (d. 1764) is said to have been the first to print in colours although Torii Kiyonobu and Torii Kiyomasu compete for the honour. The first prints were made in two colours only, red and green, in the middle of the eighteenth century. Later the gamut of colours was increased and enhanced also by blocks that imparted an embossed surface to portions of the print. The technique of sprinkling the surface with mica or metal-dust had already been employed before the introduction of colour-printing and both continued, while the use of black lacquer had only a temporary vogue.

It is not possible in the space available to refer to the work of more than a few outstanding print-makers. Kwaigetsudō, a contemporary of Masanobu, never printed in colour, but his masterly composition and line are such that the prints give the effect of a *grisaille*. They are exceedingly rare. At the same period (1700—56), the four Torii masters were producing striking and graceful prints of actors.

The first master to make full use of the possibilities of colour was Suzuki Harunobu

(c. 1725—70): his line is softer, less dramatic than those of his predecessors. He was popular and prolific. His best pupil was Kōryusai. Shunshō (c. 1726—92), the teacher of the great Hokusai, deserves mention in his own right. Twentieth-century criticism has placed Sharaku (*fl.* 1794) on a pinnacle of his own; his atrabiliary genius was not appreciated in his own time and his sure and unsparing impressions of his subjects did not sell. Kitagawa Utamaro (1753—1806) was versatile, prolific and popular. His prints of beautiful women are well known and some of his large heads are not only masterly in technique but show great intensity of feeling.

Katsuchika Hokusai (1760—1849), whose landscapes are the best-known feature of his work, was a man of astounding energy and versatility. In his old age he used to describe himself as 'the old man, mad on drawing'. Fortunately, much evidence of his delightful, witty insanity has survived. There are over three thousand Hokusai drawings *in one collection*. His *Mangwa* in fifteen volumes gives us a better picture of Japanese legend and contemporary, everyday life than any other work. His *Wave* in the *Views of Fuji* series is perhaps the best known of all Japanese prints.

A vast number of the landscapes produced by Hiroshige are well known and treasured in the West. Nearly always, the human element is more noticeable than is the case with Hokusai, and the general effect is softer. His rendering of light and atmosphere is particularly effective; his rain is very wet indeed.

Towards the middle of the nineteenth century European influences began to affect Japanese art; and a little later, the tide turned. Artists such as Whistler, Conder and many others drew inspiration from Hokusai and Hiroshige with wholly satisfactory results. Whereas the eastward current carried, with few exceptions, innovations totally allergic to Japanese standards, it brought incompatible techniques and bad pigments.

We cannot say much more of the Ukiyoe school. The 'floating world' was about to float away. Toyokuni I and his pupils Kunisada and Kuniyoshi returned to familiar scenes of Yedo, to actors and *oiran* and to legendary and historical episodes. For the last, Kuniyoshi (Plate 48) deserves special mention. From the beginning of the nineteenth century the Japanese were beginning to sense the latent menace of a strange and powerful world outside. They awoke from six hundred years of proud security to see on the horizon the sails of the 'black ships'. Instinctively they turned for help to their ancient dynasty and their ancient loyalties.

Heroic subjects from medieval history were revived by Kuniyoshi; battles of the Taira and Minamoto, a last stand of the Kusunoki in which the whistle and thud of the arrows can almost be heard. He is remarkable in having adopted the use of shadows from European art with entire success.

He was the rearguard. With mass production and diminished standards, an era passes; Japanese art can no longer be considered in isolation.

C'est glorieux, la nuit, de croire à la lumière (Edmond Rostand).

Notes on the Plates

Plate 1   Haniwa (tomb attendant). 4th—5th century. Earthenware; height 32 inches. The Hon. R.G. Erskine, London.

Plate 2   Miroku Bōsatsu (The Bodhisattva Maitreya, the 'future Buddha'). First half of 7th century. Gilded copper; height 12 inches. Author's Collection, London.

Plate 3   Gakko Bōsatsu, one of the attendants of the Yakushi Buddha. c. 720. Bronze; height 10 feet 3 inches. Yakushiji, Nara.

Plate 4   Kuze Kannon, in the Yumedono (Hall of Dreams). Asuka Period. Wood; height 6 feet 5½ inches. Hōryuji, Nara.

Plate 5   Shūkongojin, in the Hokkedō. Late Nara Period. Wood; height 5 feet 7½ inches. Tōdaiji, Nara.

Plate 6   Muchaku, a disciple of Buddha, by Unkei. c. 1210. Wood; height 6 feet 2 inches. Kōfukuji, Nara.

Plate 7   Mask for the Gigaku dance. c. 800. Wood. British Museum, London.

Plate 8   Masks for the Nō plays:

    a) Old woman (16th—17th century). Unsigned. Wood.

    b) Young woman (18th century). Signed Hōjō Taishi Kenjō.

                British Museum, London.

Plate 9   Tokonoma (alcove) arrangement:

    a) New Year poem to the Emperor Go-Tsuchimikado by Fujiwara (Sanjō) Sanetaka, an official of the court, c. 1485.

    b) Bronze vase bearing a dedication to the memory of Kōbori Enshu (d. 1648) and other tea-masters, with *kakihan* (monogram) of the former, by Seimin I, 18th century.

    c) Black Raku incense-burner, gold-flecked, 18th century.

                Author's Collection, London.

Plate 10   The Tamamushi (jewel-insect) shrine. Asuka Period. Painted lacquer on wood with gilt metal mounts enclosing beetle-wings. Hōryuji, Nara.

Plate 11   *Tenjōkoku mandara* (2 details). Temple banner depicting the reception of Shōtoku Taishi into Paradise. Asuka Period. Chūgūji Convent, Nara.

Plate 12   Panel No. 2 of the mural paintings in the Kondō which were destroyed by fire in 1949. Early Nara Period. Hōryuji, Nara.

Plate 13   Panel No. 3 (see note, Plate 12).

Plate 14   *The Ki-Fūdō* (Yellow Fūdō). 12th century painting on silk, a copy of the 9th century original. Manju-in, Kyōto.

Plate 15   *Kitano Tenjin Engi* (detail), a history of the Kitanō shrine. 13th century. Painting on paper. Kitanō Temman-gu, Kyōto.

Plate 16   *Portrait of Minamoto no Yoritomo* by Fujiwara Takanobu. c. 1200. British Museum, London.

Plate 17   Kakemono, *Akadōji*, an attendant of Fūdo. 14th century. Painting on silk. Author's Collection, London.

Plate 18   *Kirins in landscape* by Kano Eitoku. c. 1590. Two-fold paper screen. Mrs Mariquita Sedgwick, London.

Plate 19   Kakemono, *Ladies taking the air*, possibly by Nishikawa Sukenobu, but unsigned. Ukiyoe School, c. 1700. John Hudisteanu, Esq., London.

Plate 20   *White prunus*, two-fold paper screen by Ōgata Kōrin (1661—1716). Atami Museum, Tokyo.

Plate 21   *Red prunus*, two-fold paper screen by Ōgata Kōrin. Atami Museum, Tokyo.

Plate 22   Ō-yoroi (great armour), traditionally belonging to the hero Minamoto no Yoshitsune. c. 13th century. Kasuga-jinja, Nara.

Plate 23   Swords:
    a) Short sword, blade signed Sa Yasuyoshi, c. 1330, green and gold lacquer scabbard with iron mounts, dragons and waves signed Chikon, mid-19th century.
    b) Blade by Tegai Kanezane of Yamato, c. 1400.
    c) Mounts for above: guard, silver, decorated with waves, signed Masaharu, dated 1871; kurikata silver hare, signed Akimasa, c. 1810; fuchi-kashira and kojiri gold, signed Issai (Kyōto, c. 1850).
    d) Blade, signed Hasebe Kunishige (of Yamashiro), c. 1330.
    e) and f) Short sword, blade by Morimitsu of Osafune dated October 1412, inlaid brass mounts signed Yoshitoshi, c. 1850.
    b) to d) Field Marshal Sir Francis Festing, London.
    a) e) and f) Author's Collection.

Plate 24   a) Blade d (Plate 23).
    b) Blade by Akihiro, dated 1377.
    c) Blade by Yasumitsu, c. 1410, engraved à jour by Satomi Shigemitsu.
    a), b) Field Marshal Sir Francis Festing.
    c) Ex Garbutt Collection, Author's Collection.

Plate 25   Centre, top and sides: set of mounts for a sword, carp in waterfall, shakudō, signed Gōtō Denjō (d. 1712). W. W. Winkworth, Esq., London.
Bottom: fuchi-kashira, tigers on nanakō (fish roe) ground shakudō; pair of menuki to match, signed Kenyusai Naohisa, mid-18th century.
Kodzuka:
    a) Shishi in low relief on shakudō nanakō, signed Furukawa Yoshinaga, early 18th century.
    b) Horse under willow tree in silhouette, silver over shakudō, the back mi-partie gold and shakudō, inlaid copper and silver seal reading 'Nara', 18th century.
    c) Warrior knocking at a gate, inlay on fine nanakō ground of shakudō, signed Sōmin and certified by Sōyō, early 18th century. Clement Milward, Esq., London.

Plate 26   Sword-guards:
    a) Armourer's guard, pierced dragon-fly, iron, 13th century.

b) Tiger in rain, soft metal inlay on iron, signed Sadanaka, 18th century.

c) Stag in thicket, Akasaka School, iron, 16th—17th century.

d) Two courtilières inlaid on red copper, signed Sakai Yoshitsugu, c. 1850.

e) Flowers on matting, inlay on shakudō, Nara School, 18th century.

  a) Author's Collection, London.

  b) to e) British Museum, London.

Plate 27   Lacquer chest of arrows bearing the Imperial *mon*, 18th—19th century. Author's Collection, London.

Plate 28   Kettle for the tea-ceremony with fine granulation, known as Fu-ōguchi. Cast iron, with bronze lid. Nezu Art Museum, Tokyo.

Plate 29   Robe box in lacquer with silver, from the collection formed by the first Marquis Inouye. Early 10th century. Nezu Art Museum, Tokyo.

Plate 30   Writing box, evocative of the fall of blossom at Shirakawa, formerly the property of the Shōgun Ashikaga Yoshimasa. 15th century. Lacquer on wood. Nezu Art Museum, Tokyo.

Plate 31   Three lacquer boxes:

  a) Kōgō (incense box). Kamakura Period.

  b) Tea-caddy. Momoyama Period.

R. Soame Jenyns, Esq., London.

  c) Box for a tea-jar depicting a tea-master making a flower-holder. Early 17th century. Brocade, 17th century. Private Collection, London.

Plate 32   Writing-box and kōgō, both with inlay of pearl-shell and pewter on dry lacquer. School of Hōnami Kōetsu, 17th century. Iron purse, inlaid silver, 18th century, and coins of the early 19th century. Private Collection, London.

Plate 33   Ivory netsuke:

  a) Chinese landscape.   b) Sparrow.   c) Kylin.

Lacquer inro:

  d) In Somada technique, signed Tōmōtada Mitsumasa, 19th century.

  e) A love letter in makiye and pearl-shell, early 18th century.

  f) Togidashi, Yoshimitsu playing the flute on the Ashigara, signed Kōma Kwansai, 19th century.

Wood netsuke:

  g) Frog on a bucket, signed Masanao.

  h) Nō mask, signed Deme Ū-man (before 1781).

    a) to f) British Museum, London.

    g) to h) Private Collection, London.

Plate 34   Grey stoneware jar with lid, typical Dolmen ware of the 3rd—4th centuries.

Kō-seto, ovoid vase with incised pattern and greyish celadon glaze, 13th century.

British Museum, London

Plate 35   Pottery jar for leaf tea, Shidoro; produced under the patronage of Kōbori Enshu, the tea-master. Remains of original silver brocade cover, c. 1630. Author's Collection, London.

Plate 36   Tea-ceremony set: the tea-bowl, E-Karatsu fitted into lacquer box, together with Takatori caddy; blue and white spoon-holder in the style of Shonzui; bamboo whisk

1

2

3

4

5

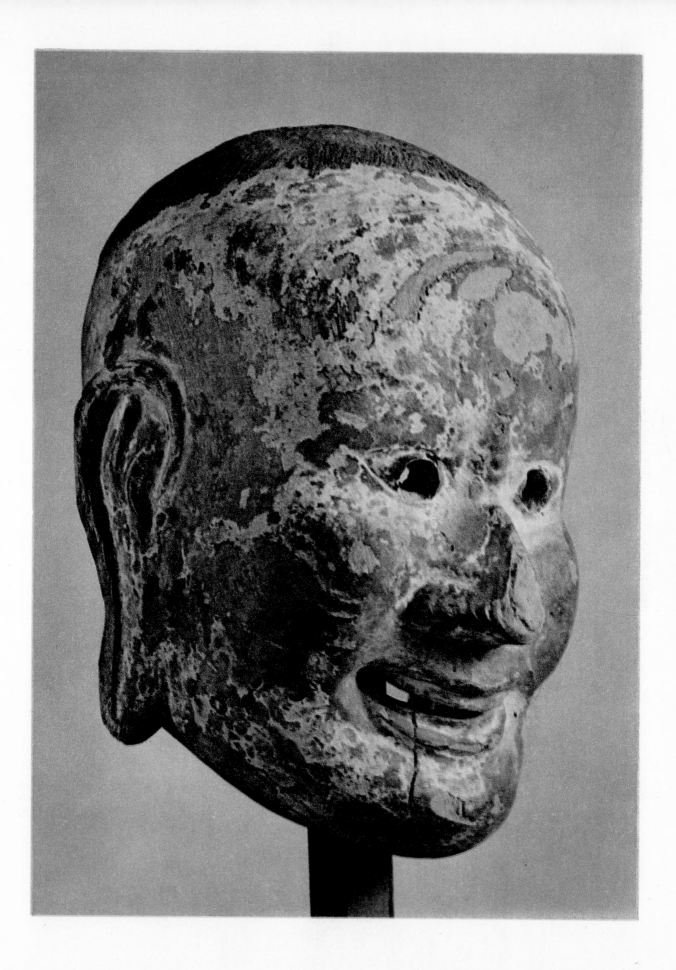

7

13

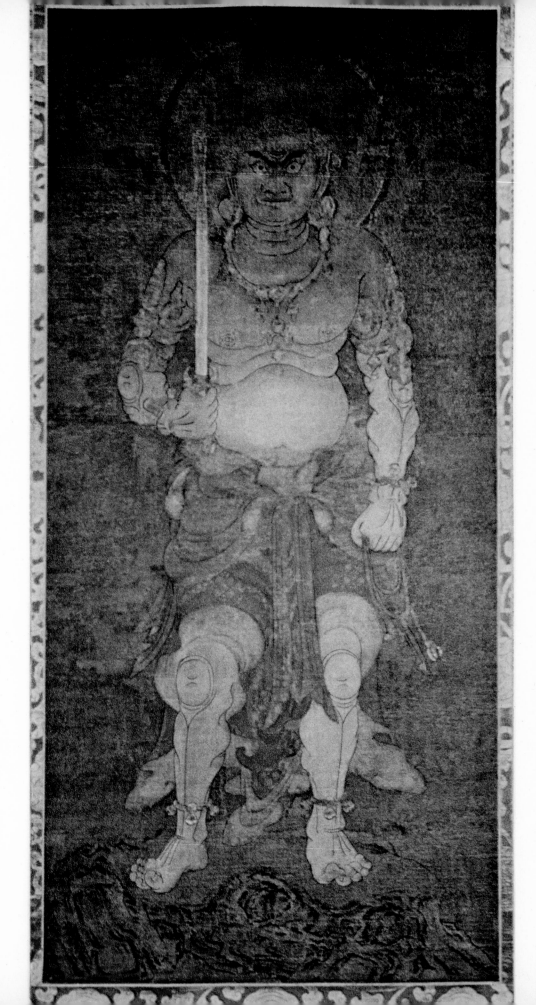

14

15

16

17

18

19

20

21

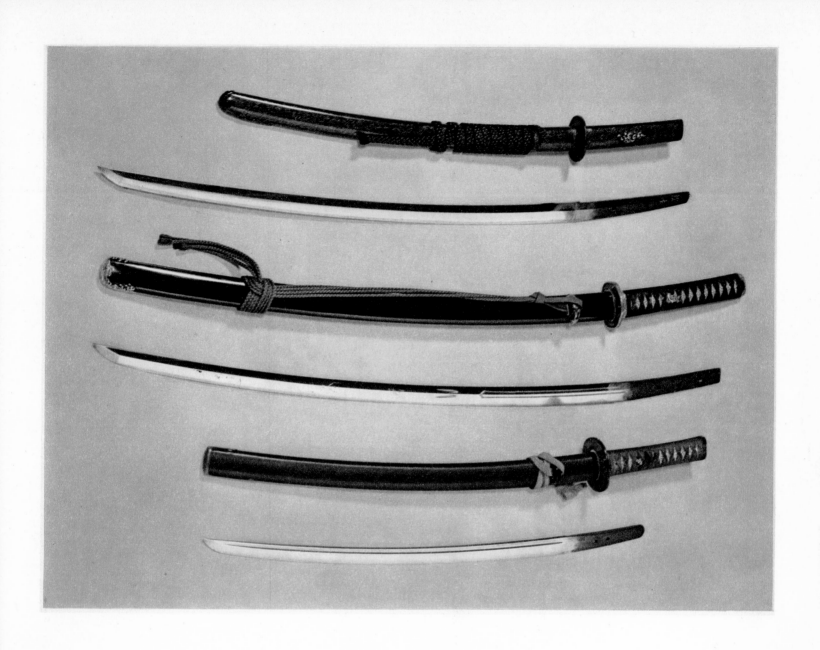

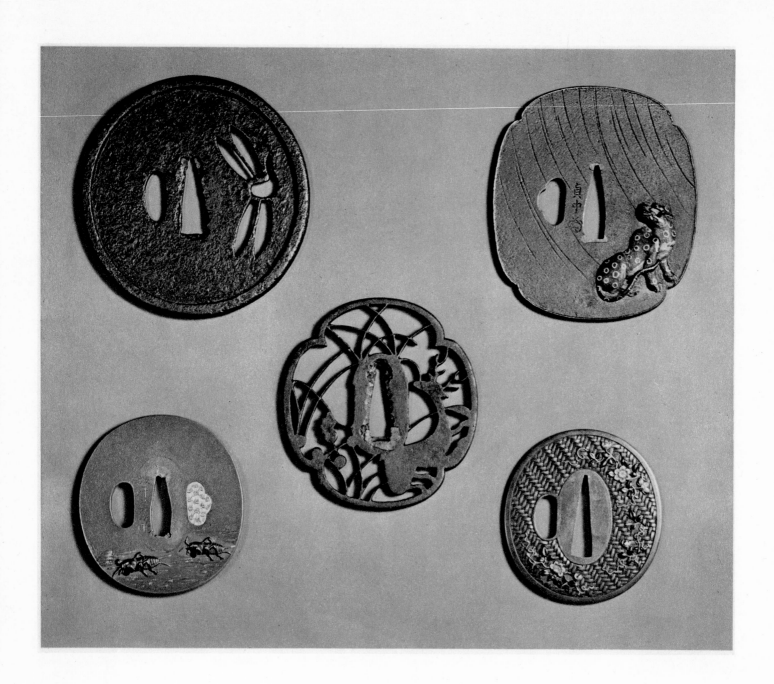

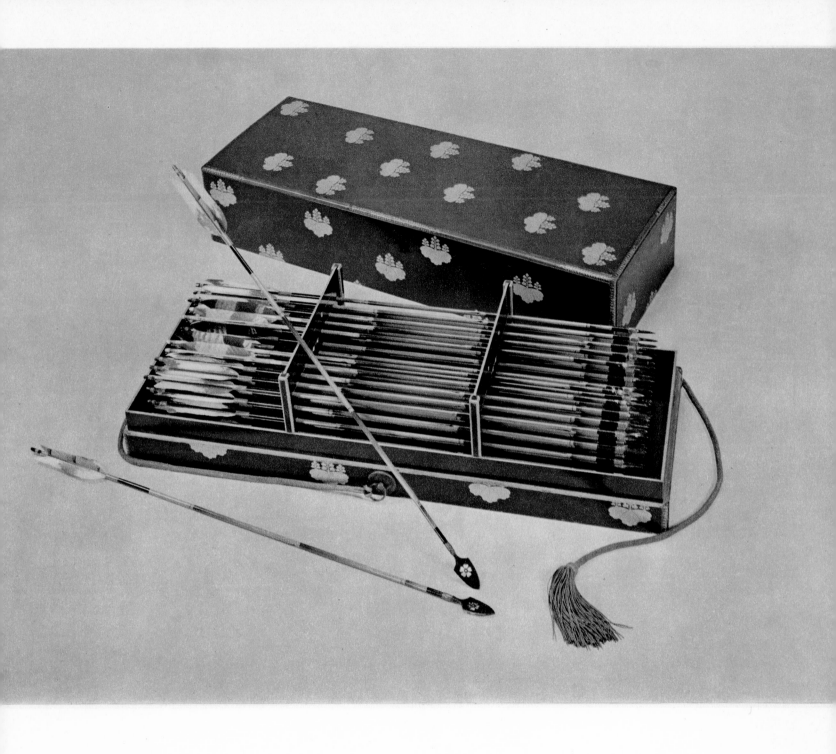

29

30

32

34

39

41

45

46

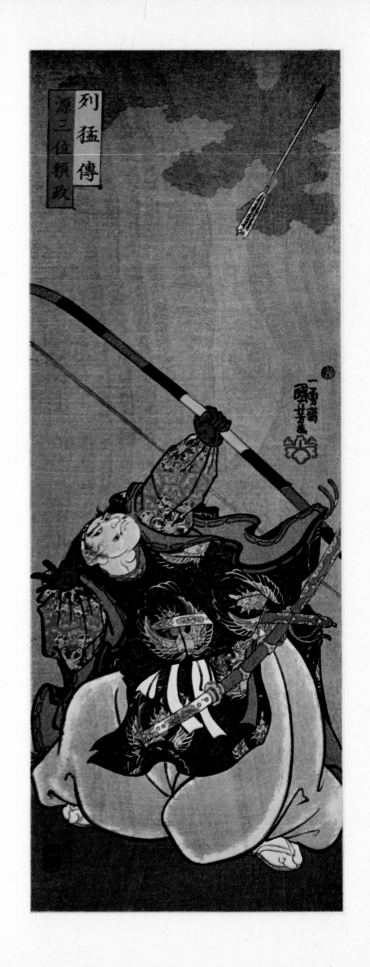

48